DOC, the Little Tractor

AUTHOR
Debbie Stofer

ARTIST
Travis Shanks

Heart to Heart Publishing, Inc.

Heart to Heart Publishing, Inc.
528 Mud Creek Road • Morgantown, KY 42261
(270) 526-5589
www.hearttoheartpublishinginc.com

Author: Debbie Stofer
Artist: Travis Shanks
Senior Editor: L.J. Gill
Co-Editor: Nicki Bishop
Designer: April Yingling-Jernigan

CPSIA Information:
Production Date: April 2018
Plant Location: Printed by Everbest Printing Co. Ltd, Nansha, China
Batch Number: 81531

First Edition
10 9 8 7 6 5 4 3 2

Heart to Heart Publishing, Inc. books are available at a special discount for
bulk purchases in the US by corporations, institutions and other organizations.
For more information, please contact Special Sales at 270-526-5589.

There are hidden hearts throughout the pages of this book.
May seeking the heart pictures serve as a reminder that Heart to Heart
Publishing, Inc desires to touch hearts through reading good books.

Please feel free to count the number of hearts on each page of the story,
beginning on page seven. It's fun!
(Answers are in the back of the book.)

This books belong to:

_____

Dear Parent and Caregivers,

Reading can be one of life's sweetest gift, and it can open doors for your child throughout his or her life. Learning and loving to read is a great accomplishment for early childhood. The following suggestions can enhance this process:

• Before reading the book, create a cozy place together and relax.

• Eliminate distractions by turning off the televisions, phones, tablets and laptops. Give your undivided attention to your child.

• Ask the child to read the title and look at the cover to predict what the story is about.

• Read with expression, enjoying this time with your child.

• Pretend to become the character and express and read the same way the character would express him/herself.

• Read a page and allow the child to repeat, mimicking your expression and inflection.

• During the reading, encourage younger children to pick out letters and older children to sound out new words they do not recognize right away.

• Help the child to use phonetic skills to sound out new words.

• Do not pressure the child if they struggle with a new word. Offer assistance. They may remember it the next time they see it. You want reading time to be a positive experience.

• Ask questions about the book, encourage discussion, and laugh together as you share the funny parts of the story. Ask "Did you learn anything new from the book? Who or what was your favorite part? What good or bad decisions were made?"

• Encourage the child to read to others, brothers, sisters, or to pretend their baby dolls or bears are their audience. They feel grown up while doing this. They can learn while assuming the role of the teacher.

Dedicated to my loves,
my granddaughter, Jayden Ann,
my son and daugher-in-law,
Joshua and Mindy,
my husband, John,
and to my loving parents,
Darrell and Joyce Francis

~ Debbie Stofer

This book is dedicated to all of my friends,
and family who support my art.

~ Travis Shanks

2 Timothy 2:6
The hardworking farmer should be the
first to receive a share of the crops.

Once there was a
little tractor named Doc

He wore tires
instead of socks!

His paint was shiny, he was sturdy and strong.

His engine sang a happy, "putt-putt" song.

9

He planted the beans,
he planted the corn.

He started working
early in the morn.

11

He hauled both round
and square bales of hay.

He worked very
hard EVERY day.

13

The days soon
turned into weeks
and the weeks
turned into months.

And Doc the little tractor
never complained,
NOT ONCE!

14

APRIL

15

Seasons passed

. . . Spring,

16

17

Summer,

18

Autumn,

20

then **Winter,**

22

And Doc's little
farm grew
bigger and
BIGGER!!!

25

Doc worked as
hard as he could
but Farmer John
understood...

That Doc couldn't
handle it all
because he was
just too small.

A bigger tractor
came to the farm.

And seeing this
caused Doc alarm!

But Farmer John
calmed Doc's fears.
He said, "Don't worry Doc
I'll keep you near."

And Doc continued
to work everyday.
He worked in his own
special way.

He did the things that he could do.

He went to the farmers market and got a new paint job too!

Because, sometimes,
you just have to be
YOU!

34

35

Note from the Author:

"Doc" the Little Tractor is written to be read to toddlers (age 1-3) and for early readers. However, it is a book that ALL ages can enjoy.

At the end of the story, you will find some fun and educational activities. Included are: Activities for Children, Interesting Farmers Market Facts and Tips for the best Farmers Market experience.

"Doc" the Little Tractor helps children to learn to be proud of who they are. It emphasizes hard work, putting forth your best effort, to not be afraid of change and that no matter what "Season" of Life you are in Spring (Youth), Summer (Adult), Fall (Middle Age) or Winter (Mature Adult) to just keep putting forth your best effort ... to do the things that "YOU" can do.

Debbie

Visit Debbie Stofer on Facebook, search Doc, the Little Tractor

Heart Answers: Page 9 - Doc's Back Wheel. Page 11 - Ear of Corn. Page 15 - Calendar Page. Page 17 - Hole on Belt . Page 19 - In the Sand Bucket. Page 21 - Hole on Belt. Page 23 - Snow Lady's Cheek. Page 27 - Heart Shaped Rock. Page 29 - In the Hay. Page 31 - Up, in the clouds. Page 33 - Doc's Wheel.

Author

Debbie Stofer is a native Kentuckian; taught college History; has a BA from Brescia; a MA from Western Kentucky University. Debbie has lived on a working farm; is the Event Coordinator at the Beaver Dam Community Farmers Market and is active in other community organizations. Passionate about art, reading, education and community, "Doc" the Little Tractor is Debbie's first children's book.

Illustrator

Travis Shanks is an artist from Western Kentucky, specializing in Watercolor Illustrations. He is an artist who aspires to inspire others with his work, and is proof that doodling in class can pay off if you follow your dreams.

Children's Activities

• Little ones can spend time identifying colors, shapes and counting.

• Encourage touching and smelling (if it is ok with the farmer); Farmers Markets equal great sensory experience.

• Let your child do the buying - let them weigh the item and handle the money.

• Do a "Rainbow Scavenger Hunt". Find an item for each color of the rainbow. For example: yellow (squash), red (strawberry), blue (blueberry). This shows a variety of colors which equals a good diet.

• Read books about Farmers Markets.

Tips for Farmers Market:
• Go early
• Bring bags
• Have cash (especially small bills)
• Let your kids pick the "best" looking produce
• Plan your meals around the Market
• Ask Farmers Markets Vendors questions
• Shop around

Farmers Market Facts

1. Farmers Markets can be open-air markets or indoor markets.

2. Farmers Markets are found in big cities and small towns.

3. Farmers Markets are usually in the mornings and on certain days.

4. You can't get "everything" all the time at the Farmers Market. There are certain seasons when products are not available.

5. The internet has changed Farmers Markets as customers from all over can keep in touch via Facebook pages and website.

6. Farmers Markets care about where the food/products are coming from ... are they from your county, your state, your country?

7. Farmers Markets are not just about retail sales ... they are about "cultivating" relationships.

8. At a Farmers Market, your fruits and veggies will be fresh as most farmers pick the produce the day before.

9. A Farmers Market is a "social" event ... bring your whole family, your friends, even your dog!

10. Farmers Markets often feature live music, arts, crafts, and all kinds of vendors ... it is like a "mini" festival.

Sources Cited on Activities/Market facts/tips
farmersmarketcoalition.org
nutrition.gov

"Doc's" Friends

Highview Farms/Crowe Family

Ohio County Farm Bureau

Beaver Dam Tourism Commission

White Gold Poultry Farm/
    Eddie Humphrey

Nikki Yandell

In Memory of Jim & Rene Humphrey

Robbie Parham Shelter Insurance

Janet Francis Head

Sweetie Dumplin's Farm

Tommy & Karen Baize

Westerfield Farms

Rickard & Vicki Alford

Marc & Elizabeth Price

Rob & Kathy Young

Belinda Welch/Sunset Ridge

Virginia Brown

Vicky Brown

Angela Porter Stewart

Linda Warren

Paisley Pig Boutique *Maverick Wallace

Louisville Grows/Louisvillegrows.org

Jinn Bug & Ron Whitehead

Kathy Terrell

Ace Inflatables

Maddie Grace Muster

Lil' G

The Kids of D. Wright Farms
    (Gracie, Tyler, Matthew & Addy)

Karen Burdin

40